BUBBLE TEA

BUBBLE TEA

50 fun recipes for boba and beyond

LIVIA ABRAHAM

photography by **ALEX LUCK**

RYLAND PETERS & SMALL
LONDON • NEW YORK

Senior Designer Toni Kay
Senior Editor Abi Waters
Editorial Director Julia Charles
Creative Director Leslie Harrington
Head of Production
Patricia Harrington

Food Stylist Livia Abraham
Prop Stylist Luis Peral
Indexer Vanessa Bird

First published in 2024 by
Ryland Peters & Small
20–21 Jockey's Fields
London WC1R 4BW
and
341 East 116th Street
New York NY 10029

www.rylandpeters.com

Text © copyright Livia Abraham 2024
Design and photography © copyright
Ryland Peters & Small 2024

Illustration credits: front cover
Twins Design studio, p.7 Tatsiana,
p.8 Microone

ISBN: 978-1-78879-585-2

10 9 8 7 6 5 4 3 2 1

Printed and bound in China

CIP data from the Library of
Congress has been applied for.
A CIP record for this book is
available from the British Library.

NOTES
* Both British (metric) and American
measurements (imperial plus US cups)
are included; do not to alternate
between the two within a recipe.
* All spoon measurements are level
unless specified otherwise. Note that
a level tablespoon (tbsp) is 15 ml and
a level teaspoon (tsp) is 5 ml.
* To sterilize screwtop jars or bottles,
preheat the oven to 160°C/150°C fan/
325°F/gas 3. Wash the vessels and their
lids in hot soapy water then rinse but
don't dry them. Remove rubber seals,
put the jars on a baking sheet and into
the oven for 10 minutes. Soak the lids
in boiling water for a few minutes
before using.
* All eggs are medium (UK) or large
(US), unless specified as large, in
which case US extra-large should be
used. Uncooked or partially cooked
eggs should not be served to the very
old, frail, young children, pregnant
women or those with compromised
immune systems.

CONTENTS

WHAT IS BUBBLE TEA?

So, what is this crazy bubble tea trend that has taken the world by storm and sees bubble tea shops popping up on every corner, some with funny cartoon-like characters in the window, some looking like colourful tea shops. Is it really true that you are eating dessert toppings and drinking tea at the same time? Yes, it is! Bubble tea is precisely that and now the whole world is eating dessert toppings and drinking tea all in one cup.

The classic bubble tea, also known as boba milk tea or pearl milk tea, is a customisable tea-based drink combined with soft, chewy, bouncy toppings that are sipped and slurped through a giant straw. This chewy beverage can be milky or fruity, and can be enjoyed hot or cold.

The original recipe from the 1980s adds tapioca pearls, commonly used to top desserts, to a classic milk tea. These pearls, also known as boba, are made from starch, which is extracted from the cassava root. These continue to be the most popular topping for bubble tea.

It is important that these pearls, and other toppings, have the perfect texture. There is a term to define this, known as Q or QQ, which means it has the perfect level of softness, springiness and bounciness. You could compare this with the way Italians swear by their pasta being *al dente* and as my strong-minded Italian father always told me, pasta that is not al dente is not acceptable. So, I can imagine that having the right Q is key to a good bubble tea for bubble tea connoisseurs. It is believed that bubble tea success is linked to a high level of Q factor and how much pleasure radiates from the experience of enjoying mouthful after mouthful of bouncy goodness that is so satisfying to many people.

Before the 1980s, desserts crowned with these bouncy toppings were very common across Asia and as adding them to drinks became more popular and widespread, the range of toppings for bubble tea broadened. As did the base drinks, which now vary from milk teas to fruit teas, to coffees and cocktails, and more elaborate and wild creations.

Bubble tea first expanded from its home in the middle of Asia before becoming a global trend that is now so popular it probably has as much of a following as coffee does. From its humble beginnings, in recent years it has even made its way into some supermarkets with kits enabling you to make bubble tea at home, so the fact that recipe books are being developed to reveal the depths and details of this drink is not surprising.

In this book, I have covered many varieties of bubble tea to give you the basic techniques learned through the simpler teas; then as you gain confidence from the more advanced teas, this will allow you to explore and experiment with your own creations. You will often find that in stores, bubble tea is made using a lot of pre-made syrups, powders and flavourings to allow for speed of service and to keep costs down.

Fat straw for boba

Cream crown topping and/ or fruit to garnish

Fruit or milk tea

Tapioca pearls (boba) and/or other toppings for texture

To differentiate from what you might get in stores, I am encouraging you to make most of the elements of the recipes from scratch so you can create every component of your drink yourself. You can, of course, choose to make some or all of these or mix it up and use some store-bought items and some home-made ones.

The main goal of this book is for you to have fun, get creative and make some colourful drinks to share with your family and friends. As a chef and someone who spends hours in the kitchen, I find that food brings people together in amazing ways and that you can get the whole family involved in creating a beautiful meal. So, I am hoping you can do the same with bubble tea and bring the family together and play with colours and bouncy, chewy ingredients and ultimately have a good laugh and enjoy some delightful drinks. I also see this as an opportunity to have a peek into the vast world of tea and introduce some teas that you may not have used or tasted before.

TOOL KIT

Here is a list of some of the tools I worked with while making the recipes. If you will be making a lot of bubble tea on a regular basis, then I recommend going through this and making sure you have most of these available. If you are only an occasional bubble tea drinker, and might only make a few recipes here and there, then I would advise picking your recipes and seeing what is needed for each one before you get started. See the note on page 4 for how to sterilize jars.

- Jugs/pitchers
- Fine-mesh sieve/ strainer
- Thermometer
- Saucepans
- Wooden spoon or heatproof spatula
- Stick blender
- Chopping board
- Sterilized jars
- Airtight containers
- Chopsticks
- Dough scraper
- Blender
- Measuring scales
- Measuring spoons/ cups
- Cocktail shaker
- Milk frother (optional)
- Piping/pastry bags
- Nozzles/tips
- Hand & electric whisks
- Set of bowls
- muslin/cheesecloth
- ice cube trays

GETTING STARTED

The first thing to decide is if you want a milky or fruity beverage. Do you like black teas and English tea with milk or are you more of a jasmine, green tea and lighter tea drinker? Black teas will be more earthy and have more body with added milk, whereas fruity teas will be lighter and often have fresh fruit, jams or purées added. You might also decide you want to skip teas altogether and use a coffee or chocolate base liquid.

Feel free to experiment with other bases, such as juices, sodas or other drinks, in combination with tea or on their own. This is the beauty of making bubble tea at home! The options are endless, and you can try anything.

Now it's time to start making the individual components. As shown on the diagram below, bubble tea has several elements, which include boba (tapioca pearls or popping boba), the tea and liquid base, the flavourings, the toppings, the crowns and milk if you are using it.

The term 'toppings' can be a bit misleading as they are often placed in the bottom of the glass, but this is the standard name for all the chewy elements added to your drink, including boba, jellies, fruit or any other toppings. Crowns or garnishes always sit on top of the drink.

It is best to make all elements first, then start assembling the drink right before you serve it. Some elements, such as jams, jellies and syrups, can be made ahead. The tapioca boba, on the other hand, will always need to be cooked fresh, although they can be prepared ahead and cooked when needed.

All the drink recipes, except the cocktails, are made for 454 ml/16 oz. glasses, topped up with ice, unless stated otherwise. The amount of liquid that fits in your glass may vary slightly depending on the size of your ice cubes. The average volume of liquid will be around 250 ml/1 cup per person, so if you are serving the drink warm, a smaller heatproof glass or cup should be used.

When making recipes with a cocktail shaker, please note that if your liquid is still warm, the shaker might pop open so it is advisable to put the ice in, add the liquid and give the shaker a gentle swirl so the ice can cool the content before you start shaking. Never put boiling or very hot liquids in the shaker.

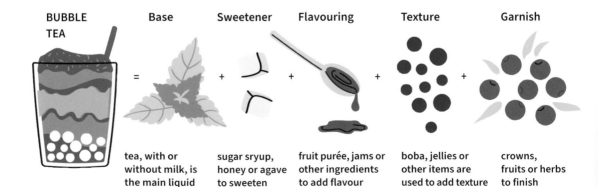

BUBBLE TEA	Base	Sweetener	Flavouring	Texture	Garnish
=	+	+	+	+	
	tea, with or without milk, is the main liquid	sugar sryup, honey or agave to sweeten	fruit purée, jams or other ingredients to add flavour	boba, jellies or other items are used to add texture	crowns, fruits or herbs to finish

SERVING A LARGER CROWD

You may want to share your bubble tea creations with a group of friends or maybe even have a bubble tea bar at a party where everyone can make their own drinks. Here are a few tips and considerations, should you want to make larger quantities or make several drinks at once.

Pick your recipes and list all the components that you need to create each drink. Calculate how much of each you will need. You can easily multiply all the recipes to make larger quantities.

Start making the components, beginning with the ones with the longest shelf life. If you are making handmade tapioca pearls, then start with these, and store them uncooked until ready to use. I would also advise using some ready-made ones, including popping boba, to diversify your offering with less effort.

Frozen ingredients for slushies can also be prepared well ahead and then just blended to order and served immediately. I would not opt for any slushies for a bubble tea bar as they will melt too quickly but could be made for larger groups and blended to order .

Move on to making the jams, followed by jellies, syrups and purées. These will all keep for at least 5–6 days if stored properly. Please refer to the individual recipes for storage details.

On the day of your event, get all the liquid bases ready, allowing enough time for the teas to cool. You can either store these in the fridge until you are ready, then build your drinks to order, or you could pre-mix some drinks, mixing teas with milks, syrups, juices and alcohols if using. When you are ready to serve, you will just need to mix these into the glasses with the toppings, ice and garnishes or give a final shake in a shaker with ice.

Prepare any garnishes as close to the event as possible, such as sliced fruit or herbs, and set aside in the fridge until ready to use. If any of the drinks have melted chocolate or syrup drizzled in the glass, then all the glasses can be decorated ahead of time and stored in the fridge.

SERVING TIPS

For larger groups, I recommended setting up a tray to contain all the glasses, then having all of your tools lined up, such as spoons, shakers, ice bowl and straws. Then organize the toppings, liquid bases and garnishes by drink, so it is all easy to assemble.

If you are creating a bubble tea bar for guests to create their own drinks, I would recommend organizing things by category. Have the base drinks in one section and then group all of the flavourings, toppings and garnishes together on individual trays or platters. This extra planning and organization at the beginning will make things much easier and more efficient later.

I would not recommend making fresh blended juice drinks, such as Head in the Clouds (see page 71) for parties as these will separate when they sit so cannot really be made ahead of time. I would also steer away from adding crowns as these will need to be made right before serving and won't hold for long. You can still make the drinks that have crowns in the recipe and just swap the crown for another garnish or just remove it.

My final tip would be, if you have time, try making the drinks you are hoping to serve at your party beforehand so you can not only taste them, but also see what preparation is involved and what might take more or less time to assemble.

THE BASE RECIPES

THE BASE TEAS

The first component of your drink will be the tea, and this will be the base of your drink. You can either use loose-leaf teas, or a teabag if you are just making one drink. I will give you suggested quantities for both options so you can choose what works best for you The recipes are a guideline so you might need to adjust the quantities and the time depending on the brand you use.

As with coffee brewing, there are recommendations on time and temperature for each different tea variety, which I will outline overleaf as a guideline, but I also suggest that you check the instructions on the pack for each tea. As the tea will be mixed in with a lot of other elements, it will lose some of its flavour so you should brew it for a minute or two longer than the packet suggests.

Whether you are a purist or just want the quickest way of doing things, you can still achieve a good tea base to make bubble tea, so how you do it will just depend on your personal preference. If you can't be bothered with the whole temperature and time thing, that is also completely fine, just make sure you always taste your tea while it is steeping. This is especially important for green teas as black tea can steep for longer before bitterness settles in. Just be careful not to burn yourself when tasting as the water will be very hot! Little by little you will get to know your teas and how far you can take them before they are too strong.

Jasmine pearls

Verveine

Butterfly
pea flower

Chamomile

Hibiscus

Genmaicha

BLACK TEA

When it comes to black tea you can use Assam, English breakfast, Darjeeling or any other black tea you like so feel free to experiment with different varieties and find the one you prefer. In general, I would use black tea as a base in milk teas due to its stronger flavour which pairs well with milk.

500 ml/2 cups water
2 tbsp loose-leaf black tea
    or 2 teabags (1 bag per serving)

Makes 500 ml/2 cups

1 Boil the water to 95°C/203°F either in the kettle or in a pan. If you don't have a thermometer, bring the water to a boil (which is 100°C/212°F), let it cool slightly and you should be good to go.

2 If using tea leaves, add to the water, stir and leave to steep for 3–5 minutes or a couple minutes more than what is suggested on the pack. Tea for bubble teas should always brewed a bit stronger than how you would usually drink it.

3 If using a teabag, add to the water in a tea cup and leave to steep for 3–4 minutes. Taste for flavour and let it steep longer if needed.

4 Strain out the tea and set aside to cool.

GREEN TEA

As with black teas, there are endless varieties of green teas. In this book I use jasmine, jencha and genmaicha as they are readily available but there are lots more you can try. Green teas are best paired with non-milk drinks such as fruit teas, soda-based drinks and some cocktails. Jasmine works particularly well with bubble tea drinks.

500 ml/2 cups water
1–2 tbsp loose-leaf green tea or
    2 teabags (1 bag per serving)

Makes 500 ml/2 cups

1 Heat the water to 80°C/176°F in the kettle or a pan.

2 Add the tea leaves and steep for 1–3 minutes. It is important you keep an eye on your green tea as it will get bitter if left for too long. I recommend tasting after a couple minutes, then leave it to steep for a bit longer if needed. As mentioned previously you will start to know how long you can go with each tea the more you practise.

3 Strain out the tea and set aside to cool.

OOLONG TEA

Oolong tea is a tea that has been partially oxidized and has a smokier taste than black tea. It is good as a base tea for milk-based recipes, but it also pairs well with fruits such as peach, pineapple, apple and pear so also works well with some fruit teas. Oolong has a flavour profile that can also withstand alcohols such as brandy, whisky or dark rum so can be a great base for cocktails.

500 ml/2 cups water
2 tbsp Oolong loose-leaf tea

Makes 500 ml/2 cups

1 Heat the water to 80°C/176°F in the kettle or a pan. Add the tea and leave it to steep for 2–3 minutes for fruit tea, 3–5 minutes for milk teas or a bit longer depending on the pack instructions. Taste for flavour and let it steep longer if needed. Strain out the tea and set aside to cool.

TEA	QUANTITY TEA	QUANTITY H2O	TEMPERATURE	TIME
BLACK TEA	2 TBSP	500 ML/2 CUPS	90–95°C/194–203°F	3–5 mins for milk tea
OOLONG	2 TBSP	500 ML/2 CUPS	80–85°C/176–185°F	2–3 mins for fruit tea
				3–5 mins for milk tea
GREEN TEA	1–2 TBSP	500 ML/2 CUPS	75–80°C/167–176°F	1–3 mins for fruit tea

HERBAL TEAS

In addition to being a caffeine-free option, herbal teas also offer another range of flavours for you to experiment with in your creations. Herbal teas work best with non-milk teas as they tend to be mild in flavour. One exception is Rooibos that also works well with milk. Using herbal teas will allow you to try something a bit different to what you might find in bubble tea shops and will give you the opportunity to create some great drinks for hot summer days.

VERVEINE, CHAMOMILE, HIBISCUS & OTHER HERBAL TEAS

All these teas can be brewed pretty much the same way. As they do not contain a lot of tannins, they won't become bitter if you let them steep for a longer time. They will need more time to develop enough flavour so that it comes through when mixed with the other ingredients. As mentioned previously, you should taste these as they steep.

Tip: You can also make herbal tea using fresh ginger or lemongrass. Place 3 sticks of lemongrass that have been bashed and sliced or about 70 g/2¾ oz. sliced fresh ginger into a pan with 500 ml/2 cups cold water. Bring to the boil and boil for at least 5 minutes. Taste and continue cooking if needed. Leave to cool before straining through a sieve/strainer.

Note: Other bases that can be used are juices, sodas or any other drink you might like to try. You can use this in combination with a tea or on their own if you prefer a tealess combo. This is the beauty of making bubble tea at home! The options are endless, and you can try anything you want to.

TEA	QUANTITY TEA	QUANTITY H2O	TEMPERATURE	TIME
VERVEINE	2 TBSP	500 ML/2 CUPS	90–95°C/194–203°F	5–10 mins
HIBISCUS	1–2 TBSP	500 ML/2 CUPS	90–95°C/194–203°F	5–10 mins
CHAMOMILE	2 TBSP	500 ML/2 CUPS	90–95°C/194–203°F	5–10 mins
BUTTERFLY PEA	1 TBSP	500 ML/2 CUPS	90–95°C/194–203°F	5–10 mins

THE SWEETENERS

The second element needed for making bubble tea is a sweetener. The most common and easiest one to make is a simple sugar syrup, which can be plain or flavoured with herbs or spices. You can also use ready-made sweeteners, such as honey or agave syrup, if preferred.

The amount of syrup you use will depend on the other ingredients in your drink and whether these are already sweetened or not. The level of sweetness will also depend on your personal taste so it is important that you always taste your drink while you are making it so you can adjust as you go.

SIMPLE SYRUP

Simple syrup is the most used type of sweetener in bubble teas and other drinks. This is the basic recipe, that you can then add flavour to if liked.

200 g/1 cup white caster/superfine sugar
200 ml/scant 1 cup water

Makes about 350 ml/1½ cups

1 Place the sugar and water in a pan. Bring to the boil, stirring occasionally until the sugar has dissolved, then simmer for a few minutes.

2 Once the sugar has fully dissolved, take it off the heat and leave it to cool completely.

3 Store in a sterilized jar or airtight container in the fridge for up to 2–3 weeks.

Food safety note: Please note that there is not enough sugar in this syrup to preserve it for a very long time so if it gets cloudy or has an unusual flavour, please dispose of it.

BROWN SUGAR SYRUP

Brown sugar syrup has a deep caramel flavour that adds an extra dimension to your drink and is a very popular addition to milk teas. Every brand of brown sugar you use will have a slightly different flavour, so you may need to experiment with a few to find the one that you like the best.

Brown sugar syrup is used to make the swirl in the glass for tiger milk teas (see page 39), and also to soak brown sugar boba and as a sweetener.

200 ml/scant 1 cup water
200 g/1 cup dark brown sugar

Makes about 350 ml/1½ cups

1 Follow the same recipe as opposite, but simmer the syrup for about 15–20 minutes until it starts thickening and has a more viscous consistency. What you are looking for is a syrup that is less runny than the normal sugar syrup so that it sticks to the inside of a glass when making tiger milk tea and it should coat your boba well. Please note the syrup will keep thickening once cooled.

FLAVOURED SYRUPS

These syrups are the same as the simple syrup recipe (see page 16) with the addition of an extra ingredient, such as a herb or spice to add flavour.

First up are herbs and fruits, but the same principle applies to spices. You can make them more or less spicy by adjusting the quantities to your liking.

MAKRUT LIME SYRUP

Makrut lime leaves (also known as Kaffir lime) have a distinct citrus note that is more floral than normal limes.

5 Makrut lime leaves
200 ml/scant 1 cup water
200 g/1 cup white caster/superfine sugar

Makes about 350 ml/1½ cups

1 Twist the lime leaves to gently tear them and release some of their natural oils.

2 Add them to the water in a saucepan and bring to the boil.

3 Simmer for a few minutes, then add the sugar. Continue simmering the syrup for about 10 minutes, stirring occasionally, then turn it off and leave it to cool completely. Once the syrup is cool you can remove the lime leaves.

4 Store in a sterilized jar or airtight container in the fridge. This should last for 1–2 weeks if stored properly.

Food safety note: The addition of herbs and spices makes these syrups more at risk of spoiling, so keep an eye on the taste and appearance and, if they start changing, it is best to dispose of the syrup and make a fresh batch.

BASIL SYRUP

This is a good way of using up the stems of herbs such as basil (or other herbs) when you have used the leaves for cooking.

10 fresh basil leaves or 2–3 stems with leaves
200 ml/scant 1 cup water
200 g/1 cup white caster/superfine sugar

Makes about 350 ml/1½ cups

1 Follow the same method as the Simple Syrup on page 16.

FRUIT SYRUP

Fruit syrups work particularly well with berries, but can also be made with other fruits.

100 g/1 cup strawberries or other berries
200 g/1 cup white caster/superfine sugar
200 ml/scant 1 cup water

Makes about 350 ml/1½ cups

1 Trim the top off the strawberries and put the fruits in a saucepan with the sugar and water.

2 Bring to the boil and then simmer for about 10 minutes, stirring occasionally.

3 Take off the heat and leave to cool down.

4 Strain the syrup to discard the strawberries and reserve in an airtight sterilized container in the fridge for up to 1 week.

Other herb and spice options include:
Thyme: 15 sprigs
Mint: 2–3 stems with leaves or 10–12 leaves
Rosemary: 1–2 sprigs
Lavender: 1 tbsp dried lavender flowers
Thai basil: 2–3 stems with leaves or 10–12 leaves
Cinnamon: 2 sticks

Lemongrass: 2 sticks (about 20 g/¾ oz.)
Cardamom: 20 pods
Ginger: 1 large thumb
Chilli/chile: 1 red chilli/chile

You can also combine herbs and spices in one syrup, such as lemongrass and lime leaf.

THE FLAVOURINGS

The next layer you can add to your drink is a flavouring in the form of a purée, a jam or fresh fruit. These are mostly used for fruit teas and introduce a huge number of possibilities for different combinations for your drinks. The beauty of making your own purées and jams is that you can use whatever is in season so you will get the richest, sweetest result and be able to experiment with different things throughout the year if you are a regular bubble tea drinker.

Purées can also be used to make ice creams or other desserts or to flavour a smoothie or a cocktail. The jams can be used for breakfast or, in certain cases, with a cheese board, so if you have a big amount of fruit to use up, I am sure it won't go to waste if you don't use all of it for your bubble tea.

THE PUREES

I always recommend tasting fruits before you start making purées as this will give you an indication of how sweet they are and if adding sugar or another sweetener might be needed. If you prefer to use store-bought purées, good brands to look for are Boirin, Monin and Funkin.

MANGO PUREE

1 ripe mango (about 400 g/14 oz.) peeled, stoned and diced (or 300 g/10½ oz. frozen mango)
juice of 1 lime (optional)
50 ml/¼ cup water (if needed)

Makes about 150–175 g/5½–6 oz.

1 Follow the method as for the Berry Purée opposite, but when checking for sweetness, also check if you might need to add some lime juice to balance the flavours.

Food safety note: If you notice anything unusual in your purées, such as mould, an off taste or smell please dispose of them immediately.

BERRY PUREE

200 g/1⅔ cups raspberries, strawberries, blackberries or pitted/stoned cherries
50 ml/¼ cup water (if needed)
honey, Simple Syrup (see page 16) or choice of sweetener (optional)

Makes about 150–175 g/5½–6 oz.

1 Put the berries in a blender. Start blending and add a little water if needed to loosen, adding 1 tablespoon at a time. Blend until you have a smooth purée.

2 Taste for sweetness and add honey, syrup or other sweetener as needed and blend again.

3 Strain the purée through a fine-mesh sieve/ strainer if liked to remove any seeds or bits that have not blended properly.

4 Store in a sterilized bottle or airtight container in the fridge for up to 1 week.

THE JAMS

The difference between a purée and a jam/preserve will be the consistency, the sugar content and how long you can keep it for. A jam should contain at least 60% the amount of sugar to fruit and it is this amount of sugar that will preserve it and allows it to be kept for longer

Making jams is a great way to use leftover fruits or very ripe fruits. As with the purées you can find a lot of lovely pre-made jams, that are perfectly fine to use.

I have used small quantities here, but feel free to make a larger batch. With small quantities there is more chance of burning the base of the pan so always make the amount listed as a minimum, stir the jam regularly and keep a close watch once it gets to the higher temperatures.

BLUEBERRY JAM

225 g/1¾ cups blueberries
135 g/⅔ cup white caster/superfine sugar
　(or 60% of the weight of the fruit used)
juice of 1 lemon (optional)

Makes about 250 g/1 cup

1 If you do not have a jam thermometer, put a couple of saucers or small plates in the freezer.

2 Put the berries in a saucepan with the sugar. Start cooking over a medium heat, stirring occasionally. As the blueberries soften, mash them with your spatula or a potato masher so they break down.

3 Use a wet pastry brush to remove any sugar that may have settled on the side of the pan.

4 When the jam bubbles vigorously, stir more regularly to avoid it sticking to the pan and burning.

5 Cook over a high heat for 15 minutes, or until the jam starts to thicken, then check the temperature. You want it to reach 104–105°C/219–221°F. Taste (taking care as the jam will be very hot) and add lemon juice if it is too sweet. If you don't have a thermometer, add a teaspoon of jam to one of the saucers from the freezer; if it wrinkles it is ready.

6 Transfer it to a sterilized jar. Leave it to cool completely before storing in the fridge.

PEACH/NECTARINE JAM

4 nectarines or peaches, stoned/pitted and chopped
60% of the weight of the fruit in caster/superfine sugar
　(e.g. 100 g/3½ oz. fruit will need 60 g/¼ cup sugar)
juice of 1 lemon (optional)

Makes about 250 g/1 cup.

1 Use the same method as for the Blueberry Jam, but weigh the fruit after it has been stoned to calculate the accurate weight of sugar.

THE TOPPINGS

What makes bubble tea unique is the amusement of sucking up the chewy components through the straw. I like to divide these into two main categories – the boba, which are the pearls that come in all colours and flavours, and then the other toppings and add-ons, which range from fruit jellies to chia seeds. All of these are available to purchase should you not want to make them from scratch.

THE PEARLS

BROWN SUGAR BOBA

These tapioca pearls can be used in most drinks as the brown sugar flavour is quite subtle and does not flavour the drink unless you mix the pearls with brown sugar syrup after they are cooked. I use both the plain version and the ones soaked in brown sugar syrup throughout the book.

70 ml/¼ cup water
50 g/¼ cup brown sugar
100 g/⅔ cup tapioca starch,
   plus extra to dust

Makes 4 servings

1 Place the water in a saucepan and bring to the boil. Add the sugar and stir to dissolve. Remove the pan from the heat, add 2 tablespoons of the tapioca starch. Mix vigorously using chopsticks or a spatula.

2 Return the pan to the heat and bring to the boil, still stirring, until the mixture starts to thicken and turn into a paste.

3 As soon as this happens, remove from the heat and add the remaining tapioca and stir.

4 Return the pan to the heat and stir vigorously to incorporate. You will end up with a flaky mixture with some loose pieces.

5 Tip the mixture onto the worktop or a large chopping board dusted with tapioca starch. The mix will still be hot at this point, so be careful not to burn yourself. If it is too hot for your hands, you can wait a few a few minutes, but no longer or it will be too hard to work with.

6 Start kneading the dough, adding a bit more tapioca if it starts sticking. You can work quite forcefully here, kneading until you have a smooth dough.

7 Cut the dough into 4 pieces.

8 Roll the first piece into a long rope about 5 mm/⅛ inch wide.

9 Use a dough scraper or knife to cut the dough into small pieces about the size of a small pea – don't be tempted to go bigger or you won't be able to suck the chewy goodness through a straw.

10 Cut the remainder of the dough into pieces, then roll each piece in the palm of your hand to make a sphere. You can leave these as more organic shapes if you do not want to roll each one.

11 Bring a saucepan of water to the boil, add the pearls to the water and cook until they float. Test one for texture and if you want them softer, keep cooking them for a few more minutes.

12 Once you are happy with the consistency, refresh them in cold water, then leave in cold water until ready to use.

Note: These will only keep for about 3–4 hours, so do not cook them too far in advance.

SWEET POTATO TAPIOCA BOBA

You can also make boba using a mix of sweet potato and tapioca. This results in a different texture to the ones made only with tapioca, with an added sweetness and flavour from the sweet potato. You can also use taro root or ube instead of sweet potato.

1 medium sweet potato
    (weighing about 150 g/5½ oz.)
100–200 g/2⅔–1⅓ cups tapioca
    starch

Makes 4 servings

1 Preheat the oven to 180°C fan/200°C/400°F/Gas 6.

2 Place the sweet potato on a baking tray lined with baking paper and pierce some holes in it with a cocktail stick/toothpick.

3 Roast the potato in the oven for about 30 minutes until it is soft and can be pierced with a sharp knife or skewer easily. Leave it to cool.

4 Once cooled, slice it in half and scoop out the insides into bowl. Add 100 g/⅔ cup of the tapioca starch and use a dough scraper to start folding the starch into the sweet potato. Mix until it is fully combined and it starts forming a dough.

5 Turn it out onto the worktop and knead slightly so that it is fully combined. If the dough feels a bit too wet, you can add a bit more tapioca starch. Keep adding starch until you have a homogenous dough that you can roll without it sticking to the surface and isn't too wet.

6 Divide the dough into 4 pieces and roll the first one into a long rope about 5 mm/⅛ inch wide. Use the dough scraper to cut the rope into roughly small pieces (small enough to be sucked up into the straw). Keep doing this until all the dough is cut, then roll each ball in the palm of your hand.

7 Bring some water to the boil in a saucepan, add the dough balls and cook for about 5 minutes or until the desired chewiness is achieved.

8 Refresh in cold water, then leave the boba in the water until ready to use. Use within 4 hours or they will start losing their shape and if the water gets cloudy, change it for fresh water. Do not store these in the fridge or they will get hard.

FRUIT BOBA

You can also make a variation of the brown sugar boba recipe on page 23 using fruit purées. These will result in fruity chewy pearls that you can make using whatever purée you want. These will be pastel in colour due to the tapioca starch, but you will still be able to taste the fruit flavour. They won't be as flavourful as popping boba, but they are worth trying, especially if you have leftover purée or juice to use up.

70 g/2¾ oz. fruit purée (see page 20) or juice
2 tbsp white caster/superfine sugar
100 g/⅔ cup tapioca starch

Makes 4 servings

1 Use the same method as for the Brown Sugar Boba (see page 23), but replace the water with purée and reduce the sugar slightly.

2 Store the boba, coated in tapioca starch, in an airtight container in the fridge for up to 1 week. You can also freeze for up to 2 months.

Food safety note: Depending on the type of purée you use, the length of time the fruit boba keeps for may vary. If you see any changes in appearance, please dispose of them. They might harden slightly in the fridge but are still fine to use.

Mango dough

Kiwi dough

Dragon fruit dough

Strawberry dough

Mixed store-bought tapioca pearls

STORE-BOUGHT PEARLS

You will find that there is a huge variety of tapioca pearls available to purchase, not only in different colours, sizes and flavours but also with different cooking times. There are even quick-cook ones that are ready in minutes. So, if you are a frequent bubble tea drinker you may opt for store-bought versions as they are quick and practical, but I do recommend you try and make the handmade ones at least once.

POPPING BOBA

Popping boba are another a great addition to your bubble tea creations. Contrary to the chewy tapioca boba, these colourful pearls have a juicy middle, so they burst in your mouth when you eat them, thus giving them their name of 'popping' boba. They come in a multitude of flavours such as lychee, rose, mango or pineapple. As they are not mixed with tapioca starch, the fruits retain their full flavour and the boba will add a punch of flavour to drinks.

They can be purchased in most Asian supermarkets or online. Popping boba can be made at home but this is quite a lengthy and more technical process, so I suggest buying them. Popping boba cannot be used in hot drinks, so for hot drinks it is best to use tapioca boba.

Kiwi

Mango

Lychee

Blueberry

Watermelon

Green apple

Strawberry

Lemon

Cranberry jelly

Mango jelly

THE JELLIES

The advantage of making your own jelly is that you can get creative and experiment with flavours that you might not find in a store. The same recipe will work with most liquids so try out some of your favourite drinks in jelly form. See opposite for a basic recipe.

As with the boba, you can purchase a huge variety of jellies in Asian supermarkets or online, so you should be spoiled for choice should you decide you don't want to make your own. Some of the popular flavoured jellies that are often available to buy are lychee, coconut, grass and konjac jelly. If you have any leftover jelly, you can add these to desserts just as they would have traditionally been used before the invention of bubble tea.

Dragon fruit jelly

Mango jelly

BASIC RECIPE FOR JELLIES

Please check the pack instructions for the agar agar as quantities and cooking instructions can differ from one brand to another. For this recipe, I used a 12 x 24-cm/4¾ x 9½-inch container. It doesn't matter if you don't have the exact size, this will only affect the thickness of the jelly. For a half recipe, I used a 12 x 18-cm/4¾ x 7-inch container.

unflavoured oil, for greasing
500 ml/2 cups fruit juice or
   other liquid of choice
caster/superfine sugar, to taste
8 g/⅓ oz. agar agar powder

Makes about 9–10 portions

1 Grease the container minimally with oil. I do this by putting a drop of vegetable oil on a piece of kitchen paper and rubbing it all over the inside of the container. You do not want the jelly to be oily, so it's important to do this with a light touch.

2 Put the juice in a saucepan with the sugar and add the agar agar. Leave it to soak for a few minutes.

3 Heat the liquid while whisking until it comes to the boil, then simmer for 3–4 minutes, whisking continuously.

4 Leave it to cool for a few minutes, then pour the mixture into the prepared container.

5 Leave it to cool further at room temperature for 15 minutes before putting it in the fridge to set completely.

6 When you are ready to use it, use a knife to cut around the edge to loosen it from the container, then flip it over onto a chopping board. Tap the base of the container gently so it pops out. If you do not want to use all of the jelly, you can also cut out the desired portion and lift out

with a palette knife or spatula. Just be careful not to scratch the container if it is metallic.

7 Slice the jelly into small cubes.

8 Store any unused jelly in the fridge in an airtight container for about 1 week.

RAINBOW JELLY

Rainbow jelly is a fun addition to your bubble tea creations, adding a pop of colour and lots of flavour. Rainbow jelly is usually made from several different flavoured jellies, cut into small cubes and mixed together. Here is a flavour combination that you can try, but feel free to experiment.

LYCHEE JELLY

250 ml/1 cup lychee juice
4 g/⅛ oz. agar agar powder
caster/superfine sugar,
    to taste

MANGO JELLY

250 ml/1 cup mango juice
4 g/⅛ oz. agar agar powder
caster/superfine sugar,
    to taste

DRAGON FRUIT JELLY

250 ml/1 cup dragon fruit
    juice
4 g/⅛ oz. agar agar powder
caster/superfine sugar,
    to taste

*Makes 4–5 portions
per flavour*

1 Cook all three jellies as per the method for the basic jelly recipe on page 29 and pour each one into a separate prepared container. Leave them to set, then cut the jellies into small cubes and mix to create a rainbow jelly.

COFFEE JELLY

This is a popular topping and can readily be found in Asian food stores or online. It is also easily made at home and this way you can control how sweet you would like to make it and how strong you would like the coffee to be. You can use filter coffee, instant coffee or any brewed coffee of your choice.

500 ml/2 cups coffee
caster/superfine sugar, to taste
8 g/⅓ oz. agar agar powder

Makes about 9–10 portions

1 Place the coffee in a pan and bring to the boil. Turn the heat down and whisk in the sugar – I recommend adding 1 teaspoon at a time when the coffee is hot and tasting it until your desired sweetness is reached.

2 Gradually add the agar agar while whisking continuously. Bring back to the boil for 1 minute, then take off the heat and leave to cool for a few minutes before pouring into a prepared container (see page 29). Leave to cool until the jelly reaches room temperature, then cool in the fridge until it is fully set and use within a week.

OTHER TOPPINGS

STICKY RICE WITH COCONUT

When in Thailand nothing beats a deliciously sweet mango paired with nutty, sticky rice drenched in a thick coconut sauce. The chewy texture of the sticky rice makes it a good addition to bubble tea if you are looking for an alternative to tapioca. If you are making this topping, then I would highly recommend buying a few ripe mangoes and making extra so you can enjoy a delicious mango sticky rice for dessert at home.

100 g/½ cup black, white or purple
   glutinous rice
100 ml/scant ½ cup coconut milk
1 tbsp caster/superfine sugar
¼ tsp salt

Makes 3–4 portions

BASIL & CHIA SEEDS

Basil and chia seeds are becoming more popular as toppings for bubble tea. With their antioxidant properties and a lot of fibre, this is a good way to include something healthy in your bubble tea creation while adding another layer of texture.

BASIL SEEDS

20 g/¾ oz. basil seeds
200 ml/scant 1 cup
   water

CHIA SEEDS

20 g/¾ oz. chia seeds
200 ml/scant 1 cup
   water

Makes 1–2 portions of each

1 Soak the seeds in the water for about 20 minutes (basil seeds) or 30 minutes (chia seeds) until they swell up, and then use straight away.

1 Rinse the rice a few times in cold water, then place in a bowl covered with more cold water and leave to soak overnight.

2 Drain the rice and transfer to a steam basket or fine-mesh sieve/strainer and steam over boiling water for about 20 minutes. Cooking times will vary between brands, so it is best to check the packet instructions and adjust the recipe accordingly, as well as tasting the rice as it cooks.

3 While the rice is cooking, make the coconut sauce by putting the coconut milk, sugar and salt in a saucepan and heating it until the sugar and salt have dissolved. Taste and adjust the sweetness if needed, then set aside to cool.

4 Once the rice is soft and fully cooked, cool it under cold water and leave it to drain. Transfer it to a bowl and combine it with the cooled coconut sauce. Store in the fridge until ready to use.

Food safety note: It is imperative to cool the rice quickly before storing it in the fridge and it is best used within 4 hours of cooking. If you want to use the rice straight after cooking, you can cool it a room temperature but please use it within 2 hours.

CROWNS

Crowns are an extra layer that can be added at the very end before serving. They bring another layer of texture and flavour and are a great way to make drinks more playful and colourful.

A simplified version I often use is just cold frothed milk made using a milk frother. It is light and airy, adding extra texture to your drink. You can even colour the foam by adding a pinch of matcha, beetroot/beet or charcoal powder straight into the milk while frothing it. It won't be sweetened so is a good option to top sweeter drinks if you want a more subtle crown. To make this crown, just froth cold milk as per the instructions of your frother as the last step of making your drink and spoon it on right before serving.

Alternatively, experiment with these richer milk, cream and cheese crowns, or even a dalgona crown (see pages 34–35) to add a touch of luxury.

CHEESE FOAM CROWN

Cream cheese topping is available in most bubble tea shops now but is often made using a cheese powder. The recipe below uses cream cheese instead of a powder and will give a rich cream foam to top your drinks. The addition of sea salt will make this topping salty to contrast beautifully with sweeter bubble tea drinks.

50 g/¼ cup cream cheese
50 g/¼ cup double/heavy cream
2 tsp caster/superfine sugar
pinch of salt

Serves 1–2

1 Whisk the cream cheese with the cream, sugar and salt until it is firm and fluffy and holds its shape, but do not over-whisk it or it will become hard to spoon on. You are aiming for a soft peak here, so not as firm as the whipped cream opposite. Taste it and add more sugar if needed.

2 As with whipped cream, the mix will firm up a bit more as it sits. If it gets too stiff, you can loosen it with a little milk or cream just before serving.

Note: Add any additional flavouring or colouring when you first start mixing the cheese and cream.

CREAMY MILK FOAM CROWN

100 ml/scant ½ cup whipping cream
50 ml/scant ¼ cup full-fat milk
2 tsp evaporated milk
1 tsp caster/superfine sugar
¼ tsp salt

Serves 2–3

1 Whisk all the ingredients together until you have a smooth cream that holds a gentle shape. Don't expect to get firm peaks here the way you would when whipping cream to a stiff peak. The ratio of milk to cream means that the cream will always remain somewhat soft, but that is exactly what you want so you can spoon a graceful dollop on top of your drink.

2 Make this crown right before serving as it will start to soften with time.

WHIPPED CREAM CROWN

100 ml/scant ½ cup double/heavy cream
1 tsp honey or another sweetener
flavouring of choice (optional)
few drops of food colouring (optional)

Serves 2

1 Whisk the cream with the honey in a bowl with a hand whisk until you have stiff peaks (a firm cream that will hold it shape and does not flop over).

2 You can test the firmness of your cream by taking a small dollop on a spoon and seeing if the peak stays up or if it folds over. If it folds, it is still too soft

so carry on whisking (being careful not to over-whisk it or it will become grainy). Set aside in the fridge until you are ready to top your drink.

3 The easiest way to apply this cream top is with a piping/pastry bag and nozzle/tip. Spoon the cream into the piping bag and pipe on top of your drink. If you are planning just to spoon the crown on, then it is best to whisk it a bit less.

Note: The cream will continue firming as it sits. If it firms up too much, you can loosen it by stirring some more cream in right before serving.

Other toppings:
Egg custard is another popular topping available in bubble tea shops. It is often made using egg-flavoured pudding powder mixed with water. If you want to use it at home, you can use pre-made flan, crème caramel or egg pudding powders or make these from scratch. There are several recipes available online for all of these.

Candy floss/cotton candy and **marshmallow fluff** make interesting toppings and are easy to get hold of.

Ice cream is another easy-to-use option.

MATCHA DALGONA CROWN

Matcha dalgona is a light and airy crown, that adds texture and dimension to your drinks. This is a good alternative to the coffee version opposite if you are not a coffee drinker.

1 tsp matcha green tea powder
1 tsp hot water
1 egg white
1–2 tsp caster/superfine sugar
few drops of lemon juice

Serves 1–2

1 Mix the matcha powder with the hot water to make a paste.

2 Whisk the egg white with the matcha paste along with 1 teaspoon of the sugar and a few drops of lemon juice.

3 After a few minutes taste and see if you are happy with the sweetness. If not, add more sugar.

4 Continue whisking until the egg is fluffy and holds its shape and the matcha is fully integrated.

Note: If you do not want to use the eggs, you can substitute this for the liquid from a 400-g/14-oz. can of chickpeas (the liquid is known as aquafaba) for a vegan version.

COFFEE DALGONA CROWN

Dalgona coffee was invented in Korea and has now become popular globally. This crown is perfect for using on a Dalgona Iced Coffee (see page 76).

1 tbsp instant coffee
2–3 tsp caster/superfine sugar
1 tbsp boiling water

Serves 1–2

1 Put the sugar, instant coffee and boiling water in a bowl. Whisk with an electric whisk until the mixture is light and fluffy and holds its shape. This can take a while depending on how powerful your whisk is.

Note: Make this right before serving as it will not hold its shape for long.

BUBBLE TEA RECIPES

MILK TEAS

Here are recipes for my favourite milk teas and the ones that I keep coming back to. As with brewing tea, the strength of the milk tea you enjoy will be personal to you, so the amount of milk added can be adjusted to your liking. Additionally, the type of milk used is a recommendation only but feel free to use any milk you prefer, even plant-based options.

BASIC MILK TEA

This is a basic milk tea recipe that can be unsweetened or sweetened and can therefore be a neutral base for many bubble tea creations. There are numerous versions of simple milk teas from country to country so you can easily substitute this for a Hong Kong milk tea, Singapore milk tea or any other milk tea recipe you come across. They are all similar, but some are more sweetened than others and some use creamer or evaporated milk instead of dairy milk. Ultimately, what you want is a milk-to-tea ratio that works for you. I personally like mine quite strong so I only add a small amount of milk.

250 ml/1 cup black tea
    (see page 14)
75–100 ml/¹⁄₃–½ cup milk
    or plant-based milk
    (or more to taste)
sweetener, to taste
2–3 tbsp boba or jelly
    of choice
ice cubes

Serves 1

1 Combine the freshly brewed tea with the milk.

2 Add sweetener, mix and taste, then adjust as needed.

3 Place boba or jelly in the glass and fill with ice.

4 Top with the milk tea.

TIGER MILK TEA

Tiger milk tea gets its name from the stripes of brown sugar syrup drizzled around the inside of the glass before pouring in tea, or from the 'tiger sugar' that is used to make this drink in bubble tea shops. The brown sugar adds sweetness and a distinct caramel flavour to the tea. It is important that the brown sugar syrup is viscous enough to coat the glass if you are using a home-made syrup. You can also purchase ready-made tiger sugar online if you prefer.

250 ml/1 cup black tea (see page 14)
75–100 ml/⅓–½ cup milk or plant-based milk sweetener, to taste
2–3 tbsp Brown Sugar Boba (see page 23)
50–70 ml/¼–⅓ cup Brown Sugar Syrup (see page 16)
ice cubes

Serves 1

1 Combine the freshly brewed tea with the milk.

2 Sweeten if needed, but as you will be adding the brown sugar boba you might prefer to keep it unsweetened.

3 Mix the brown sugar boba with half the brown sugar syrup, then spoon them into the bottom of the glass.

4 Drizzle the remaining sugar syrup around the inside of the glass while rotating the glass, to create tiger stripes.

5 Fill the glass with ice and top with the milk tea.

Note: If the tea is still slightly warm, you can combine the milk and tea in a cocktail shaker with ice, give it a swirl to cool the liquid down, then shake before you pour into the glass.

THAI TEA

This is another favourite of mine, which I drink day in and day out when I am in Thailand, which is why I have included it here. It has a distinctive flavour and reddish colour, often due to the addition of food colouring, but I have been told by some Thai friends that sometimes tamarind paste is also added to the tea to enhance the colour. Personally, I always use store-bought Thai tea bags as they tend to be more concentrated and are just as good as making it from scratch. Thai tea is available in most Asian shops.

50–100 ml/¼–½ cup milk

2–3 tbsp condensed milk

2–3 tbsp boba of choice

ice cubes

200 ml/scant 1 cup Thai tea (made from a store-bought Thai teabag)

Serves 1

1 Mix the milk and condensed milk together until fully combined and taste. You can use more or less milk – some people like Thai tea with just condensed milk and some like it in combination with milk, so start with a small quantity of milk and add more if you like.

2 Place the cooked boba in the base of a glass and top with ice. Pour in the cooled tea and top with the milk. Stir to combine and taste.

3 If you find the tea is not sweet enough you can always add some more condensed milk and give it a good stir again.

CHAI MILK TEA

3-cm/1¼-inch piece of fresh ginger, washed and sliced

6 cardamom pods, bashed

1 cinnamon stick

4 peppercorns

1 star anise

5 cloves

500 ml/2 cups water

2 tsp Darjeeling tea or black tea of choice (or 1 tea bag)

100 ml/scant ½ cup milk

1 tbsp honey or another sweetener

4–5 tbsp boba and/or toppings of choice

ice cubes (optional)

Serves 2

I have added a chai recipe so you have a spiced milk tea base. There are lots of variations of chai tea, from the karak chais in the Middle East to the masala chais in India.

1 Place the sliced ginger with the other spices in a saucepan with the water and bring to the boil.

2 Turn the heat down and simmer for 5–6 minutes.

3 Add the tea, then simmer for another 3–4 minutes.

4 Add the milk and the sweetener and taste the tea to see if it is strong enough for you or if you would like to simmer it further.

5 Once you are happy with the flavour, strain the mixture and set aside until ready to use.

6 If you would like to drink it hot, then serve right after straining with your choice of toppings. If you would like to drink it cold, then leave it to cool down and serve over ice with your choice of boba and toppings.

Note: Feel free to adjust the of spice to suit your taste.

TARO MILK TEA

This purple drink is very popular in bubble tea shops and can be made using taro powder. The purple colour of this drink makes it a fun base to use if you want to create a colourful and playful drink. You will get a vibrant purple colour if using the taro powder and a much paler colour with the fresh taro root (see below for how to use this). Ube, another root similar to taro, tends to be more purple.

Creamy Milk Foam Crown
  (see page 32) (optional)
2–3 tbsp Brown Sugar Boba
  (see page 23) or boba
  of choice
ice cubes
2–3 tbsp taro powder
150 ml/²⁄₃ cup black tea
  (see page 14)
100 ml/scant ½ cup milk
1 tbsp condensed milk
  (optional)
blueberries, to serve
  (optional)

Serves 1

1 First, prepare the Milk Foam Crown and set aside.

2 Put the cooked boba in a glass and add some ice.

3 Combine the taro powder and tea in a blender with a couple of ice cubes and blend until fully combined. If you like your drink very sweet, you can add some condensed milk to sweeten.

4 Pour into the glass and add the milk.

5 Top with the prepared milk crown and serve immediately, topped with blueberries if liked.

Note: If you do come across fresh taro root, I would recommend boiling it with the skin on and not trying to peel it before cooking, as the skin can be very irritating for some people. Once it is soft and a cocktail stick/toothpick can go in easily, drain it, leave to cool, then cut in half and scoop out the flesh.

LATTES

Lattes are just another variation of milk teas but usually have a higher ratio of milk than milk teas. You can reduce the amount of milk if you prefer though. These can be enjoyed hot or cold so I have included instructions for both in the recipes.

MATCHA LATTE

Matcha latte has now become a staple in many coffee shops as an alternative to coffee. The quantities used in this latte are a guideline only and can be adjusted to your personal taste.

Matcha Dalgona Crown (see page 34)

2–3 tbsp Brown Sugar Boba
(see page 23)

1½–2 tbsp Brown Sugar Syrup
(see page 16) (optional)

1–2 tsp matcha green tea powder,
plus extra to decorate

1 tsp hot water

100–150 ml/scant ½–⅔ cup
cold water

ice cubes

150–200 ml/⅔–scant 1 cup cold
or hot milk

Serves 1

1 First make the Matcha Dalgona Crown and set it aside.

2 Combine the brown sugar boba with the brown sugar syrup in a small bowl, or leave the boba as they are if you prefer your drink unsweetened.

3 Put the matcha powder in a jug or glass with the hot water and mix well with a spoon or small whisk until you get a paste. Add the cold water and whisk until well combined.

4 Add the mixed brown sugar boba and syrup to a glass and top with ice. Pour in the milk, then add the matcha paste.

5 Top with the Matcha Dalgona Crown and sprinkle with matcha powder to finish.

Note: If you think your drink is not sweet enough, you can add some plain sugar syrup or more brown sugar syrup. If you would like to drink this hot, use hot water and milk instead of cold.

TURMERIC LATTE

Turmeric latte is a warming drink that packs a punch with its vibrant yellow colours and distinct turmeric flavour mixed with other spices. It holds its own without the need to add much more so I recommend enjoying this with brown sugar boba.

1 tsp ground turmeric

½ tsp ground cinnamon,
plus extra to decorate

½ tsp ground ginger

2 cloves

1 tsp vanilla extract

100 ml/scant ½ cup water

400 ml/1⅔ cups milk

1–2 tbsp honey

4–5 tbsp Brown Sugar Boba
(see page 23)

Serves 2

1 Put the spices and the vanilla in a saucepan with the water and bring to the boil.

2 Simmer for a few minutes, then add the milk and honey. Simmer for another 2–3 minutes, whisking to create some foam. If you would like a thicker foam, you can use a hand frother.

3 Taste for sweetness and adjust if needed.

4 Place boba in the base of a glass, top with the latte and sprinkle with cinnamon to serve.

Note: If you would like to serve this cold, turn off the heat and leave it to cool slightly. Transfer to a shaker with some ice and let it cool a bit more with the ice. Give it a good shake, then serve over ice with your choice of boba.

RED BEAN MATCHA MILK TEA

A popular combination in some bubble tea shops is to combine the red bean latte (see below) and matcha latte into one drink. The sweetness of the red bean paste pairs well with the bitterness of the matcha and it's also fun because you can layer it.

1 tsp matcha green tea powder
1 tsp warm water
100 ml/scant ½ cup cold water
1½ tbsp red bean paste and/or
    30 g/1 oz. sweet red beans
ice cubes
200 ml/scant 1 cup milk or
    plant-based milk
1–2 tsp sweetener of choice
2–3 tbsp Brown Sugar Boba
    (see page 23) or boba of choice

Serves 1

1 Combine the matcha powder and warm water in a small jug or glass. Mix well with a spoon or small whisk until you get a paste. Add the cold water and combine, then set aside.

2 Put the red bean paste and/or red beans in the base of a glass and fill the glass with ice.

3 Combine the milk with the sweetener.

4 Pour the milk into the glass and then the matcha. Stir to combine and taste for sweetness. Adjust if needed. You can garnish with more red beans or any other topping you would like. Serve immediately.

RED BEAN LATTE

Red bean paste is made from the adzuki bean, commonly used in desserts from Japan, China and Korea. It has a sweet and nutty flavour and gives you a full-bodied drink when blended with milk. The red bean paste is already slightly sweet and so are the brown sugar boba, so leave the sweetener out if you prefer less sweet drinks.

2 tbsp red bean paste
150 ml/⅔ cup milk or plant-based
    milk (coconut milk works well)
100 ml/scant ½ cup black tea
    (see page 14)
sweetener (optional)
2–3 tbsp Brown Sugar Boba
    (see page 23) or boba of choice
ice cubes
red beans, to decorate (optional)

Serves 1

1 Put the red bean paste in a blender with the milk and tea and blend briefly to combine. Taste for sweetness.

2 Put the brown sugar boba in the bottom of a glass and then fill the glass with ice.

3 Pour in the mix from the blender and top with red beans or your choice of topping.

Note: If you prefer you can also make this recipe without the tea and just add 100 ml/scant ½ cup milk or adjust the tea quantity to your liking.

PLANT-BASED MILK TEAS

Though all the previous milk recipes can be substituted with plant-based milks, I also wanted to have a few recipes that are created purely as plant-based drinks. As with the milk teas, you can still substitute the plant-based milks with regular milk, with the exception of the horchata on page 50, where you are actually making the rice milk in the recipe.

STRAWBERRY MILK TEA

Strawberry milk tea reminds me of drinking sugary strawberry milk during my childhood. In this version, the addition of tea makes it less sweet and the colour is more subdued. This allows for the addition of fresh fruit and more sweet toppings.

2–3 tbsp Brown Sugar Boba
(see page 23)

ice cubes

5–7 fresh strawberries, diced

150 ml/²⁄₃ cup jasmine tea

100 ml/scant ½ cup plant-based
milk of choice

2–3 tbsp Strawberry Syrup
(see page 18)

Serves 1

1 Put the boba in the base of a glass with some ice and 3–4 of the diced strawberries.

2 Combine the tea, milk and strawberry syrup in a blender and blend for a few minutes. Taste and adjust the sweetness if needed.

3 If you want the milk to be more pink you can add a couple of strawberries and blend again.

4 Pour the tea into the glass and top with a few more strawberries.

Note: You can also use store-bought strawberry milk and substitute it for the plant-based milk. Make sure you check the label as it may have sugar already added.

THE COCOMANGO

This drink is inspired by the mango sticky rice dessert, which is one of my favourites. The chewy and nutty flavour of the rice is a great alternative to tapioca pearls if you want to try something different and it gets coated with a sweet coconut sauce for added sweetness. One key thing here is to pick a ripe and good-quality mango as this will make all the difference to the result of your bubble tea. If the mango is very hard, it is most likely not ripe and will not be sweet enough.

150 ml/²⁄₃ cup Thai tea
(made with 1 Thai tea bag)

1 tbsp condensed milk

1 fresh mango, peeled, stoned and
cut into cubes small enough to
go through a straw

100 g/3½ oz. Sticky Rice (see page 31),
made with purple rice if possible

100 ml/scant ½ cup coconut milk

ice cubes

Serves 1

1 Brew the tea and let it cool.

2 Put the condensed milk in the bottom of a glass. Add the diced mango (reserving a little for a garnish), followed by the Purple Rice.

3 Fill the glass with ice and pour in the tea.

4 Top with coconut milk and garnish with diced mango.

THE WHITE LADY

Spain, Mexico and many other Latin American countries, all have versions of horchata. It was brought from Spain to its colonies where it was then adapted using local ingredients. One main difference is the kind of nut or seed that is used. In Spain, tiger nuts are used, in Mexico it is made with rice, but it can also be made from sesame seeds, melon seeds, gourd seeds and even some herbs. Here, I am sharing a delicious recipe made with rice that I think everyone should try, with or without boba.

2–3 tbsp Brown Sugar Boba
    (see page 23)
30–50 ml/scant ¼ cup
    Brown Sugar Syrup
    to taste (see page 16)
ice cubes

HORCHATA

100 g/3½ oz. jasmine rice
500 ml/2 cups water
50 g/1¾ oz. blanched
    almonds
1 tsp ground cinnamon,
    or more to taste
1 tsp vanilla extract
3 tbsp condensed milk,
    or more to taste
pinch of sea salt (optional)

SUGAR RIM

1 tsp ground cinnamon
1 tbsp caster/superfine sugar
water, honey or sugar syrup,
    for dipping

Serves 1

1 First, make the horchata. Rinse the rice and combine it with the water and the almonds and let it soak for at least 3–4 hours at room temperature or overnight in the fridge.

2 After the rice has soaked, transfer it with the liquid to a blender with the cinnamon, vanilla, condensed milk and salt and blend until the rice has broken down.

3 Strain through a fine-mesh sieve/strainer or cheesecloth/muslin over a colander. Taste and adjust the sweetness and cinnamon quantities if needed.

4 Reserve in the fridge until ready to use. This will keep refrigerated for 2–3 days in a bottle or sealed container.

5 Mix the cinnamon and sugar for the cinnamon sugar rim and put on a plate. Put some water, honey or sugar syrup on another plate. Dip the rim of a glass into the water, then dip it into the cinnamon sugar and turn a few times until the entire rim is evenly coated. Lightly tap the glass before turning over to remove any excess.

6 Mix the brown sugar boba with half the brown sugar syrup and add it to the base of the glass. Top with ice and fill with the horchata.

7 Drizzle the remaining syrup over the top before serving.

FRUIT TEAS

Fruit teas are the second main category of bubble tea and can be made with most fruits. In shops, they are often paired with green tea and made using jams or syrups and fresh fruit, but this is kept to a minimum for cost and time reasons. I have tried to include as much fresh fruit as possible, paired mostly with home-made syrups and using different teas, including a herbal tea to inspire you to try different things. All these recipes are perfect for warmer weather and for entertaining so try some of them when you have guests over for a barbecue or garden party.

PASSION FRUIT & PEACH TEA

Peach iced tea is such a popular drink now, so I wanted to create my own version. I have used sencha green tea here as it has a slightly more grassy and earthy flavour, which pairs well with the peaches. Feel free to replace it with any other green tea you have available if you prefer though. I used a mix of peach jam and fresh peach here, but you could use just fresh peaches if they are in season and very ripe. Just muddle them with the lime to get lots of juice out of them and adjust the sweetness if needed.

1 ripe peach or nectarine

2–3 tbsp green tea boba or boba of choice

ice cubes

1 passion fruit

juice of ½ lime

75 ml/⅓ cup passion fruit juice (I used Rubicon passion fruit juice)

175 ml/¾ cup sencha green tea

1 tbsp peach jam (store-bought or homemade, see page 21)

½–1 tsp Simple Syrup (see page 16) (optional)

Serves 1

1 Dice half the peach or nectarine and slice the other half. Reserve a few slices and cubes for a garnish.

2 Put the green tea boba in the base of a glass with the sliced peaches and top with ice and half of the passion fruit seeds.

3 Muddle the diced fresh peach with the lime juice and the other half of the passion fruit seeds in a cocktail shaker.

4 Add the passion fruit juice, green tea and ice and shake for a few minutes. Taste and adjust the sweetness if needed. Shake again for 30–60 seconds.

5 Pour the drink into the prepared glass and garnish with the reserved peach.

Note: If you would like this drink to have a spicy kick, use a Chilli Syrup (see page 19) to sweeten instead of simple syrup, and garnish with half a chilli/chile.

STRAWBERRY, VERVEINE & BASIL TEA

When strawberries are in season, they are one of my biggest pleasures and their natural sweetness is such a treat. They are a perfect pair to basil, which I combine them with regularly in desserts and salads, so I wanted to create a drink version to enjoy. I found that the lemony herbal notes of verveine tea pair exquisitely with strawberries and, in combination with the basil syrup, this is a thirst-quenching drink with the perfect amount of sweetness from the syrup and fresh fruit.

2–3 tbsp Brown Sugar Boba (see page 23) or boba of choice

2–3 tsp soaked Basil Seeds (see page 31) (optional)

2–3 strawberries, hulled and quartered, plus a few extra to garnish

ice cubes

2 tbsp Strawberry Purée (see page 20)

250 ml/1 cup verveine tea

2 tbsp Basil Syrup (see page 18)

4–6 fresh basil leaves or sprigs, to garnish

Serves 1

1 Put the boba in the bottom of a glass with the soaked basil seeds, if using.

2 Add the strawberries and top with ice.

3 Put the strawberry purée, verveine tea and basil syrup in a cocktail shaker with a few cubes of ice and shake for 30–60 seconds until all the ingredients are combined and chilled.

4 Pour the drink into the prepared glass and top with some more chopped strawberries and garnish with sprigs of basil.

Note: You can also top with some jelly or other garnish of choice.

LEMONGRASS, MAKRUT LIME & MANGO TEA

This drink is inspired by a trip to Bali, where I was offered a delightfully refreshing lemongrass drink on the beach. It was basically just a lemongrass syrup with sliced fresh lemongrass, lots of ice and some sparkling water, but it was a revelation to me. It was such a simple drink, delicious and refreshing and different, and I couldn't believe that it had not occurred to me to make lemongrass syrup at home. I have paired it with Makrut lime leaves and mango – a match made in heaven.

2–3 tbsp Brown Sugar Boba (see page 23) or boba of choice
ice cubes
½ mango, peeled, stoned/ pitted and diced
2 tbsp lemongrass syrup (see page 19)
juice of ½ lime
3 Makrut lime leaves, chopped, plus 1 extra leaf to garnish
250 ml/1 cup jasmine tea

Serves 1

1 Put the boba in the base of a glass. Add some ice and the diced mango (reserving a small amount to garnish).

2 Put the lemongrass syrup, lime juice, chopped lime leaves and the jasmine tea and some ice into a cocktail shaker and shake for 30–60 seconds, so all the ingredients are combined and nicely chilled. Taste and adjust sweetness if needed.

3 Pour the mix into the glass and top with the rest of the diced mango and garnish with a lime leaf.

PINK GRAPEFRUIT, LYCHEE & POMEGRANATE TEA

On its own, lychee can be quite sweet, so I have combined it with grapefruit to balance the sweetness. Add the grapefruit gradually as it's slightly bitter and you may prefer to use less, but the pomegranate will in turn balance the bitterness.

2–3 tbsp lychee boba and/or Rainbow Jelly
   (see page 30) (optional)
ice cubes
2 tbsp fresh pomegranate seeds
1 small pink grapefruit – half juiced,
   the other half sliced and quartered
150 ml/⅔ cup jasmine tea
100 ml/scant ½ cup lychee juice (I used Rubicon)
sweetener, to taste

Serves 1

1 Put the lychee boba and/or rainbow jelly in base of a glass. Add ice cubes, the pomegranate seeds and the grapefruit slices.

2 Combine the tea with 20 ml/4 teaspoons of the grapefruit juice and the lychee juice in a cocktail shaker with some ice. Shake for 30–60 seconds and check the taste. You can choose to add more grapefruit juice or a sweetener at this stage if liked.

3 Pour the tea into the glass and garnish with rainbow jelly and more pomegranate seeds.

Note: You can also use hibiscus tea for this drink as another herbal tea option.

BUBBLE TEA SLUSHIES & SMOOTHIES

Slushies are fun to make on a really hot summer's day to quench your thirst. The difficulty with making slushies at home is that you often need to add a lot of ice while blending to get the slushy consistency and this tends to water down the taste. One solution is to freeze the juice or fruit ahead of time so you can blend these into a slushy rather than adding all the extra ice. Therefore, some of the recipes here will have to be started at least the day before you want to make them.

For the smoothies and slushies, you may need to make a larger quantity, depending on your blender and how much it needs in it for the blades to work successfully, so I would recommend doing at least a double portion. This is especially true for the layered drinks that require two different mixtures if you are using a standard blender. Thermomixers and high-speed blenders can sometimes work with smaller quantities so if you know yours can, feel free to try a single serving rather than a double one, but I have made all the recipes in this section double.

LEMON BUTTERFLY SLUSHY

Butterfly pea flowers are blue and make a vibrant blue tea with a uniquely earthy and woody taste. When mixed with anything acidic, such as lemon or lime juice, the tea turns purple making a fun and colourful drink.

juice of 2–3 lemons
(about 50 ml/scant ¼ cup)
650 ml/2¾ cups water
2–3 tbsp Simple Syrup
(see page 16) or to taste
100–150 ml/½–⅔ cup
butterfly pea tea
4–5 tbsp lemon or raspberry
popping boba
100 g/¾ cup fresh or frozen
raspberries, chopped

Serves 2

1 The day before you want to drink your slushy, make the lemonade by combining the lemon juice, water and simple syrup in a jug/pitcher. Taste for sweetness and acidity from the lemon juice and adjust to your taste.

2 Freeze 400 ml/1⅔ cup of the lemonade in ice cube trays and reserve the rest in the fridge in a sealed container for the next day.

3 Brew the butterfly pea tea, leave it to cool, then reserve in the fridge in a sealed container.

4 Once the lemonade cubes have frozen and are ready to use, put the popping boba in the base of 2 glasses, and then spoon in the chopped raspberries. If you are using frozen raspberries, you might need let them thaw slightly before chopping. Set the glasses aside until needed.

5 Put half the lemonade ice cubes in a blender with a little of the leftover lemonade just to loosen, then start blending. Gradually add the lemonade as needed until you get a slushy consistency. How much you need will depend on your blender but you should need most of it. Taste for sweetness and add more simple syrup if needed. Reserve the lemon slushy in a jug in the freezer while you make the butterfly pea lemonade.

6 Put the remaining lemonade ice cubes in the blender and add a little butterfly pea tea just to loosen, then blend to a slushy consistency. As before, add the tea as needed and taste for sweetness.

7 Once both slushies are made, put the lemon slushy in your glasses, then top with the purple butterfly tea lemonade slushy and serve immediately.

WATERMELON & CUCUMBER SLUSHY

Make this slushy when watermelon is at its prime as it will make a huge difference to the flavour. Usually, watermelon season starts in late spring but it will depend on where you live. This is perfect to make for a large group as you can buy one big melon, chop it up and freeze it, then blend with the other ingredients right before serving.

400 g/14 oz. watermelon, cut into ice cube-size cubes, plus a slice to garnish
200 ml/scant 1 cup jasmine tea
½ cucumber, peeled (about 150 g/5½ oz.)
4–5 fresh mint leaves
juice of 1 lime
2–3 tbsp Simple Syrup (see page 16), or to taste
4–5 tbsp Brown Sugar Boba (see page 23) or boba of choice

Serves 2

1 The day before you want to drink your slushy, cut the watermelon into cubes (reserving a slice to use as a garnish, stored in the fridge wrapped in damp paper towel) and put them in a freezer bag and freeze. Try to keep the cubes in a flat layer so they don't stick together in one big block, which will make them harder to blend.

2 Make the jasmine tea, leave it to cool and store in a sealed container or bottle in the fridge.

3 When you are ready to make the slushy, put your choice of boba in 2 glasses.

4 Peel and cut the cucumber into big chunks.

5 Put the frozen watermelon cubes in a blender with half the jasmine tea, the mint leaves, lime juice and cucumber. Start blending and add more jasmine tea if the blender needs more liquid to work. Blend until you get a slushy consistency. Taste and adjust the sweetness – how much sugar you need to add will depend on how sweet your watermelon is.

6 Pour the slushy into the glasses and garnish with a slice of watermelon.

PINEAPPLE & COCONUT SMOOTHIE

Pineapple and coconut are a match made in heaven. I have added some mango jam for added sweetness and some turmeric, which not only enhances the colour but will also add some flavour. If your pineapple is very sweet, you can also choose not to use the mango jam. I have used two kinds of pearls here to show how you can combine multiple pearls in one drink, but using just one kind also works well.

4–5 tbsp mango popping boba and/or store-bought mini green pandan pearls or other mini tapioca pearls

PINEAPPLE LAYER

300 g/10½ oz. frozen pineapple (or fresh pineapple cut into cubes and frozen)

150 ml/⅔ cup black tea

3 tbsp mango jam (shop-bought, or follow the method on page 21)

¼ tsp ground turmeric

COCONUT LAYER

200 ml/scant 1 cup coconut milk

2–3 tbsp Ginger Syrup (see page 19)

6–10 ice cubes

Serves 2

1 If using a fresh pineapple, cut the pineapple into cubes, place in a freezer bag and in the freezer for a few hours until frozen, or overnight. Make sure you reserve a slice to garnish and some pineapple leaves if you would like to use them.

2 Once the pineapple is frozen, prepare the pandan tapioca pearls as per the pack instructions.

3 Place the frozen pineapple in a blender with the tea, mango jam, turmeric and 5-6 ice cubes. How many you need will depend on your blender so start by adding three, then keep adding until you get a slushy consistency. Taste and adjust the sweetness. Pour into a jug/pitcher and set aside in the freezer.

4 For the coconut layer, place the coconut milk in the blender with the ginger syrup and 5-6 of the ice cubes until you have a slushy consistency. If the mixture is too liquid, add a couple more ice cubes and blend again. Just bear in mind that the more ice you add, the more the drink will lose flavour, so add ice gradually. The coconut layer will be slightly more liquid than the pineapple so don't worry if you don't get exactly the same consistency for both.

5 Put your choice of boba in the base of 2 glasses and add the pineapple slushy. Combine the coconut slushy with the pandan tapioca pearls and add to the glasses. Garnish with a slice of pineapple and/or some pineapple leaves if you want.

MATCHA & RASPBERRY SMOOTHIE

This smoothie is on the less sweet side, with the earthy, grassy and slightly bitter notes of matcha contrasting with the sweet and sour notes of the raspberry. The matcha and raspberries work really well together to create a refreshing smoothie.

2–3 tbsp raspberry popping
    boba or Brown Sugar Boba
    (see page 23)

MATCHA LAYER

2–3 tsp matcha green tea
    powder
2–3 tsp hot water
150 ml/²/₃ cup almond milk
    or other plant-based milk
2 tbsp condensed milk
1 banana
6 ice cubes

RASPBERRY LAYER

150 g/5½ oz. frozen
    raspberries, plus extra
    to garnish
½ banana
150 ml/²/₃ cup almond milk
    or other plant-based milk
ice cubes
condensed milk or
    sweetener, to taste

Serves 2

1 First, prepare the matcha layer. Combine 2 teaspoons of the matcha powder with the hot water in a small bowl and mix to a paste.

2 Place in a blender with the milk, condensed milk, banana and ice cubes and blend until it is well combined and becomes a slushy consistency. If the mix is too watery you will need to add a few more ice cubes (bearing in mind that the more ice you add, the more the drink will lose flavour, so add ice gradually). Taste for sweetness and add some more condensed milk if needed. You can also add some more matcha powder if you think it is not strong enough. This is all down to personal taste.

3 Pour the mixture into a jug/pitcher and set aside in the freezer.

4 Rinse the blender and make the raspberry layer. Blend the frozen raspberries, banana and 100 ml/scant ½ cup of the milk with 4–5 ice cubes. Gradually add more milk if the mixture is too thick or add more ice cubes if it is too runny.

5 Taste and add some condensed milk if needed. Raspberries can vary quite a lot in terms of sweetness or sourness, so it is best to add condensed milk at this stage rather than at the beginning so you can see how it tastes once blended. Set aside in the freezer until needed.

6 When ready to assemble your drink, put the boba in the bottom of a glass. Add some frozen raspberries, broken into pieces. Spoon the matcha layer into the glass and add a few more raspberry pieces. Add the raspberry layer and garnish with more raspberries.

INDULGENT TEAS

This drinks in this section are designed to be bold and bright and make a statement. They are there for you to have fun with and play with different crowns, toppings and garnishes. They are the most elaborate recipes in the book as they contain more components, but as mentioned previously, do not let this discourage you from trying them. You will have made some of the individual base recipes earlier in the book and if not, they are all approachable and completely doable at home.

BLUE MOON

This recipe uses butterfly pea flower tea again, but without any acidic elements this time, so it will keep its vibrant blue colour and make for a showstopper drink with the addition of candy floss/cotton candy as a garnish. The combination of lavender and blueberries make this an original drink so it's definitely one worth creating for guests. I love the blueberry jam so I would recommend making extra if you like blueberries so you can enjoy it later on toast.

200–300 ml/1–1½ cups freshly brewed butterfly pea tea

2–3 tbsp Blueberry Jam (see page 21)

4–5 tbsp Taro or Brown Sugar Boba (see page 23)

ice cubes

100–150 ml/½–⅔ cup milk or coconut milk

1–2 tbsp Lavender Syrup (see page 19)

blue candy floss/cotton candy, to garnish

Serves 2

1 Start by making the butterfly pea tea, then leave it to cool.

2 When you are ready to build your drink, put the blueberry jam in the bottom of 2 glasses, followed by the boba. Top with ice.

3 Combine the milk and the lavender syrup in a cocktail shaker with some ice. Shake for a minute and check for sweetness, adjust, then pour into the glasses.

4 Top with the butterfly tea. Do not fill all the way to the top if you are using the candy floss. You want some ice to be sitting above the tea because the candy floss will dissolve in seconds when in contact with liquid, but it can sit on the ice for a couple of minutes.

5 Garnish with candy floss and serve immediately.

TROPICAL DRAGON

This bright pink drink contains dragon fruit powder (also known as pitaya powder), which is now considered a superfood. Though dragon fruit can sometimes be bland if it's not in season, the powder is very flavourful and works well combined with milk and tea, so do try it even if dragon fruit is not your favourite.

2 tbsp mango jam
  (shop-bought, or follow
  the method on page 21)
100 g/3½ oz. Cheese Foam
  Crown (see page 33)
ice cubes

SUGAR RIM

¼ tsp dragon fruit powder
1 tbsp caster/superfine sugar

TEA

300 ml/1¼ cups milk or
  plant-based milk
200 ml/scant 1 cup jasmine tea
2–3 tbsp dragon fruit powder
1–2 tbsp Simple Syrup
  (see page 16) or more
  to taste (optional)
4–5 tbsp Brown Sugar Boba
  (see page 23) or other
  boba of choice

GARNISH

Mango Jelly (see page 29)
fresh fruit of choice (kiwi,
  dragon fruit or any
   tropical fruit will work)
dehydrated dragon fruit
  pieces (optional)

Serves 2

1 Begin by making all the different components, starting with the mango jelly so it has time to set. Then make the mango jam, the simple syrup and the tea.

2 Once you are ready to start building the drink, start by preparing the glasses. To make the sugar rim, mix the dragon fruit powder with the sugar on a saucer. Put some water on another saucer and dip the rim of 2 glasses in the water first and then into the sugar, rotating the glass until the rim is evenly coated. Give the glass a slight tap before flipping it over to remove any excess. Save the leftover sugar for the tea.

3 Make the Cheese Foam Crown and set aside.

4 Spoon some mango jam into the base of the glasses and add your choice of boba.

5 Use a long spoon to spread some of the Cheese Foam Crown inside one side of the glass to create a pattern. Top the glasses with ice.

6 Place the milk, tea, leftover sugar from the rim and the dragon fruit powder in a blender and blend until combined. Taste for sweetness and adjust.

7 Pour the blended mixture into a cocktail shaker with some ice and shake for 30–60 seconds and then pour into the prepared glasses. Finish with another layer of Cheese Foam Crown and top with fresh fruit.

HEAD IN THE CLOUDS

Honeydew is a popular flavour in bubble tea shops so I wanted to include it here. It is very important that you use ripe honeydew so don't be tempted to make this when melon is not in season or the drink will require a lot of sugar. I have used multi-coloured mini pearls here to make it more fun, but feel free to use any pearls you like. You should be able to find a variety of coloured pearls online or in Asian food shops.

½ honeydew melon
(350 g/12½ oz.), cut
into cubes
150 ml/²/₃ cup jasmine tea
1–2 tsp Simple Syrup (see
page 16) or more to taste
4–5 tbsp sago pearls or
mini tapioca pearls
ice cubes
2 scoops of matcha ice
cream

Serves 2

1 Place the honeydew, tea and sugar syrup in a blender and blend until combined. Adjust the sweetness if needed and pass through a sieve/strainer to make it as smooth as possible.

2 Place your boba of choice in the base of 2 glasses and top with ice. Make sure you have ice all the way to the top as this will help support the ice cream.

3 Put the blended tea in a cocktail shaker with some ice and shake for 30–60 seconds, then pour into the glasses. Be careful not to overfill the glasses if you are going to top with ice cream.

4 Finish with a scoop of matcha ice cream. This will be a bit of a balancing act, so place it on top gently.

THE BARBIE

This is definitely a drink where you can get creative with your toppings and add sprinkles and sparkles to your heart's content. The wilder, the better in my opinion, so have fun with it.

Whipped Cream Crown
   (see page 32)
ice cubes

STRAWBERRY SAUCE

400 g/14 oz. fresh or frozen
   strawberries
50 ml/scant ¼ cup water
2 tbsp caster/superfine sugar

TEA

150 ml/⅔ cup black tea
100 ml/scant ½ cup milk
2 scoops of strawberry
   ice cream
8–10 strawberries, hulled
   and cut in half, plus extra
   to garnish (start with less)
Simple Syrup (see page 16),
   to taste

TO GARNISH

4–5 tbsp strawberry popping
   boba or other boba
   of choice
sprinkles
sugar-coated mini
   doughnuts (optional)

piping/pastry bag and
   nozzle/tip

Serves 2

1 Start by making the strawberry sauce. Place the strawberries in a saucepan with the water and sugar. Cook for a few minutes until they soften, then mash so they break down.

2 Cook for another 5–6 minutes, then pass through a sieve/strainer, pushing through with a ladle, to make a smooth sauce.

3 Return the strained sauce to the pan and simmer for another 10 minutes or until it has thickened. The sauce should coat the back of a spoon and stay in place, not run. If the mix is still too thin, you can return it to the pan and reduce it some more. Leave to cook completely before using in the drink.

4 Next, make the Whipped Cream Crown. Spoon it into a piping/pastry bag with a nozzle/tip and set aside in the fridge until needed.

5 Blend the tea, milk, ice cream and strawberries in a blender until smooth. Taste for sweetness and adjust if needed.

6 Put the boba in the base of the glasses, then spoon some strawberry sauce around the inside of the glasses, rotating as you go. Fill with ice.

7 Pour the strawberry mixture into the glasses.

8 Top with the Whipped Cream Crown and decorate with sprinkles, a sugar doughnut, if using, or more strawberry sauce if you want.

BOBA COFFEES & CHOCOLATES

Bubble tea has become so popular since it was first invented that now boba is not only put in teas but also in coffees, chocolate drinks and even cocktails and desserts. So in this section I have included some recipes that are not tea-based so you can explore something different and also have some options to make some non-tea based drinks should you want to.

VIETNAMESE COFFEE

I have spent a lot of time in Vietnam over the years – it has become one of my favourite places to visit and I try and head there at least once a year. My latest go-to place is An Bang beach in Hoi An, a small beach town where time stops and everyone is friendly. Days start very early there, and sunrise is one of the busiest times of day on the beach as most locals go for a swim or some exercise or even some karaoke before it gets too hot. So it's a great way to start the day, sitting and sipping on an iced Vietnamese coffee, watching the world go by.

For this recipe, I have used a traditional Phin filter, which is the one used in Vietnam. You can order it online or find it in some Asian supermarkets, along with the Vietnamese coffee. I like to use Trung Nguyen brand of coffee as I have seen it on numerous occasions in Vietnam and it tends to be readily available abroad, but any other brand of Vietnamese coffee will work too. If you do not have a Phin filter you can use a French press or a coffee filter, but the coffee won't be as strong as when using a Phin filter.

2 tbsp Vietnamese coffee
80–100 ml/⅓–½ cup boiling water (depending on how you are brewing it)
2–3 tbsp Brown Sugar Boba (see page 23)
ice cubes
50 ml/scant ¼ cup condensed milk, or to taste
Coffee Jelly (see page 30)

Serves 1

1 Place the coffee in the Phin filter.

2 Add in a little bit of boiling water, then push down the filter lid and compress the coffee gently.

3 Add more boiling water to the top of the filter and let the coffee drip until all the water has passed through.

4 While the coffee is dripping, add the boba to a glass and fill with ice.

5 Once the coffee is ready, pour it into a blender with the condensed milk and some ice and blend until fully mixed.

6 Pour into the prepared glass and top with cubes of coffee jelly.

DALGONA ICED COFFEE

This creamy coffee is easy to make and the dalgona top adds some excitement to the drink

Coffee Dalgona Crown (see page 35)
50 ml/scant ¼ cup brewed coffee
   or a double shot of espresso
150 ml/⅔ cup milk or coconut milk
2 tsp Simple Syrup (see page 16),
   or more to taste
2–3 tbsp Brown Sugar Boba (see page 23),
   mixed with 2-3 tbsp Brown Sugar
   Syrup (see page 16) to taste
ice cubes

Serves 1

1 Firstly, make the Coffee Dalgona Crown.

2 Put the boba in the base of a glass with the simple syrup. Fill the glass with ice.

3 Pour in the milk, followed by the coffee.

4 Top with a few spoonfuls of Coffee Dalgona Crown to finish.

ICED CARAMEL LATTE

If you like caramel, then this one is for you as it has layer after layer of caramel in different forms.

Whipped Cream Crown (see page 32)
150 ml/²⁄₃ cup milk or plant-based milk
100 ml/scant ½ cup brewed coffee
    or 1 double shot of espresso
4 tsp caramel sauce, plus extra for
    drizzling
2–3 tbsp Brown Sugar Boba (see page 23)
    mixed with 2–3 tbsp Brown Sugar
    Syrup (see page 16)
small caramel fudge pieces, to garnish
    (optional)
ice cubes

Serves 1

1 Prepare the coffee and set it aside to cool.

2 Make the Whipped Cream Crown and set aside in the fridge.

3 Put the boba in the base of a glass.

4 Put the milk, coffee, caramel syrup and 4–5 ice cubes in a blender and blend for a few minutes until the ice has broken down. Taste and adjust the sweetness.

5 Swirl some caramel syrup around the inside of the glass, if liked, then fill the glass with ice.

6 Pour in the blended coffee and top with a few spoonfuls of the Whipped Cream Crown.

7 Drizzle more caramel sauce on top and garnish with small fudge pieces.

ICED OREO & CHOCOLATE SHAKE

This creamy cross between a bubble tea, milkshake and sundae is perfect for a sweet treat.

Whipped Cream Crown (see page 32)
    (optional)
2–3 tbsp Brown Sugar Boba
    (see page 23) or boba of choice
ice cubes
4 oreos
100–150 ml/½–²⁄₃ cup black tea
50–100 ml/¼–½ cup milk of choice
1 scoop of vanilla ice cream, plus
    1 scoop to garnish (optional)

WHITE CHOCOLATE & OREO RIM (OPTIONAL)

50 g/1¾ oz. white chocolate
2 oreos, biscuits/cookies only, crushed

Serves 1

1 First, prepare the chocolate rim for your glass. Melt the chocolate in the microwave or over a double boiler. Place the crushed oreo biscuits on a saucer. Dip the rim of a glass into the melted chocolate and then into the oreo crumb, swirling around to coat evenly. Tap the glass slightly to remove any excess before turning it over.

2 Prepare the Whipped Cream Crown, if using, and set aside in the fridge.

3 Put the boba in the base of the glass and fill with ice.

4 Place the oreos, black tea, milk and ice cream in a blender with a few ice cubes and blend until well combined.

5 Pour into the prepared glass. Top with a scoop of vanilla ice cream, if using, and some of the oreo crumbs left from coating the glass.

6 You can also drizzle the remaining white chocolate over the top if you want it to be even more indulgent.

CHOCO MARSHMALLOW FLUFF

As someone who grew up in Switzerland, hot chocolate was usually a mug of rich melted chocolate to be enjoyed by the fire in cosy fluffy socks, with a dog or a little sister curled up next to me, or in a chalet or cafe hideout when your nose and toes are frozen and all you want is to duck in somewhere warm and drink something soothing. Personally, I have always found that I am too full after drinking one of those pure chocolate drinks and prefer a chocolate drink made from cocoa powder and milk. For this recipe I use the latter and add just a little bit of melted chocolate to make it slightly indulgent!

This recipe can be used either hot or cold, so feel free to drink it hot if you prefer but here, I have made an iced version. If you are drinking it hot the chocolate swirl in the glass won't stay so you can drizzle some chocolate over the marshmallows at the end instead.

100 g/3½ oz. dark chocolate, plus extra to garnish
250 ml/1 cup milk
1 tbsp cocoa powder
1–2 tsp Simple Syrup (see page 16) (optional)
2–3 tbsp Brown Sugar Boba (see page 23), or more to taste
ice cubes
2–3 tbsp marshmallow fluff
mini marshmallows, to garnish (optional)
blow torch (optional)

Serves 1

1 Melt the chocolate in a glass bowl set over a pan of simmering water (making sure the base of the bowl doesn't touch the water), or in the microwave.

2 Spoon some of the melted chocolate into a glass and swirl to decorate the inside. Place in the fridge to set.

3 Heat half the milk in a pan or in a jug/pitcher in the microwave and combine with the remaining melted chocolate and the cocoa powder. Whisk until all the chocolate is incorporated and add the rest of the milk to cool it down.

4 Whisk until everything is combined. Feel free to add more milk at this stage if you want to.

5 Place the boba in the base of the chilled glass and top with some ice.

6 Pour in the chocolate mix, making sure not to overfill so it doesn't spill over when you top with marshmallow fluff. You can blowtorch the fluff to caramelize it, if liked.

7 Top with mini marshmallows to finish.

Note: Marshmallow fluff is very sticky so I found the easiest way to get it to stay in place is to make sure it connects with the rim of the glass. If you push it towards the rim it will stick to it and then you can keep adding more on top.

BOBA COCKTAILS (& MOCKTAILS)

As popular as bubble tea has become, it is not surprising that the delicious chewy tapioca pearls have now made their way into cocktails. With the amount of flavoured boba and popping boba now available, you can add them to a wide variety of cocktails and mocktails. I have shared some alcoholic and non-alcoholic cocktails in this section to cover all tastes. For the alcoholic ones, the recipes will also work without the alcohol if preferred and I have also suggested alcoholic pairings for the non-alcoholic ones.

COOL AS A CUCUMBER

Years ago, my partner came up with a cocktail. As a true Irish man, he loves a good party and coming up with new cocktails to impress our friends. This Zen martini, as he called it, had cucumber, lime and mint as the stars of the show. This version works really well with the addition of popping boba.

½ a large cucumber

1 green apple

juice of 1 lime

3–4 tbsp apple popping boba or other boba of choice

10 fresh mint leaves, plus a sprig to garnish

1–2 tbsp Simple Syrup (see page 16), or to taste

50–80 ml/¼–⅓ cup gin

200 ml/scant 1 cup jasmine tea

ice cubes

Serves 2

1 Start by making the cucumber and apple garnishes. Cut 2 strips of cucumber using a vegetable peeler and lay out flat on a plate or baking sheet covered with some damp paper towel. For the apple garnish, cut 2 thin slices of apple, brush with a little lime juice to prevent them from browning and set aside with the cucumber.

2 Juice the remaining cucumber and apple in a juicer if you have one, or blend it in the blender and strain through a fine-mesh sieve/strainer.

3 Place your choice of boba in the base of 2 glasses.

4 Put the lime juice in a cocktail shaker with the mint leaves, simple syrup, gin, cucumber and apple juice, tea and some ice cubes. Shake for 30–60 seconds, then taste and adjust as needed. I have left the alcohol quantity flexible here as you may like this more or less strong so I would recommend starting with a smaller amount and adding more if you prefer.

5 Pour into the prepared glasses and garnish with the apple slices, cucumber strip and a mint sprig.

PEACH ME UP

Peaches are another one of my favourite fruits when they are in season and at their prime, especially that first bite of the first deliciously ripe one I devour. The juice always tickles down my chin because they are so perfectly ripe and extra juicy and the sweetness sends my taste buds into a frenzy. My favourite peaches are Italian ones, as I grew up with my Italian father eating them throughout the summer. This recipe is far from Italian, with the addition of yuzu and genmaicha tea, but the versatility of peach allows for unexpected pairings and these work really well together.

1 fresh peach

2–3 tbsp Basil Syrup (see page 18), or more to taste)

300 ml/1¼ cups genmaicha tea

70-100 ml/scant ½ cup vodka

2–3 tsp yuzu juice

ice cubes

2–3 tbsp peach popping boba

fresh basil leaves, to garnish

Serves 2

1 Cut a few thin slices from the peach and set aside to garnish your finished drinks.

2 Dice the rest of the peach and put it in a cocktail shaker with the basil syrup. Muddle to break down the peach, then add the tea, vodka, a small amount of yuzu and some ice and shake for 30–60 seconds. Taste and adjust the taste if needed, adding more yuzu if its not citrusy enough for you.

3 Put the peach boba in the base of 2 glasses, fill with ice and add in a few basil leaves. Pour in the drink and garnish with the reserved peach slices.

GINGER PASSION

Ginger originated in south-east Asia and was one of the first commodities to be widely traded, finding its way as far as classical Greece and Rome. In this recipe, I pair the spice of the old mighty ginger, with the tartness of passion fruit and the smokiness of oolong tea to create a subtle but complex drink. The apple juice should be added gradually so you can taste as you go.

4–5 tbsp Brown Sugar Boba (see page 23) or boba of choice
1 lime
handful of fresh mint leaves, plus extra to garnish
2–3 tbsp Ginger Syrup (see page 19)
300 ml/1¼ cups oolong tea
50–100 ml/¼–½ cup apple juice, or to taste
3 passion fruits, halved
ice cubes

Serves 2

1 Put the boba into the base of 2 glasses.

2 Cut the lime into small pieces and place in a cocktail shaker. Add the mint leaves and ginger syrup and muddle together with the lime.

3 Add the tea, half the apple juice, the pulp of one passion fruit to the cocktail shaker and give it a stir and taste. Adjust the taste by adding more apple juice or any of the other ingredients as needed. Set aside.

4 Fill the glasses with ice and spoon in the pulp of half a passion fruit and some mint leaves into each glass.

5 Add ice to the shaker and shake for 30–60 seconds.

6 Pour the drink into the glasses and garnish with half a passion fruit.

Note: You could add dark rum or brandy if you want an alcoholic version as they go well with oolong tea.

TEA BUDS OF SPRING

In this cocktail I use rhubarb and elderflower – spring flavours that suggest that the long cold nights are finally behind us and it's time to start celebrating with some bright, refreshing floral drinks in the company of some rays of sunshine and the blooms that are appearing in the garden. You could top up with Prosecco or sake instead of elderflower tonic for a boozy version.

4 strawberries, hulled and cut into small chunks or slices, plus extra to garnish

50 g/1¾ oz. strawberry boba or boba of choice

ice cubes

300 ml/1¼ cups jasmine tea

20 ml/4 tsp Rhubarb Syrup (ready-made or see recipe on page 20) or purée

100 ml/scant ½ cup elderflower tonic

candied rhubarb ribbons (see Note opposite), to garnish

Serves 2

1 Place the strawberries in the bottom of 2 glasses with the popping boba and top up with ice.

2 Combine the jasmine tea with the rhubarb syrup or purée in a cocktail shaker with some ice and shake vigorously for 30–60 seconds. Taste and adjust the sweetness if needed.

3 Pour into the prepared glasses and top up with elderflower tonic. Garnish with candied rhubarb ribbons or a strawberry.

Note: To make candied rhubarb, peel rhubarb into thin strips using a vegetable peeler, and place on a baking sheet lined with baking paper, in a single layer. Brush both sides with simple syrup (see page 18) and cook in a low oven preheated to 90°C/194°F until they are dry. Check after 10–15 minutes, noting that some strips will cook faster than others. Once the strips are dry take them out of the oven and wrap each strip around a wooden spoon or other utensil and leave to dry. Work quickly as it won't work if the strips cool down too much. If the strips crack they are too cooked; and if they stick and don't curl they need to cook for longer.

POPSICLES

Making popsicles is a great way to use up any leftover purées or juices you have. The recipe below can be used with any flavour or fruit purées you have to use up. See page 91 for some other flavour suggestions, or just get creative with whatever you have to hand and make some new exciting fruity iced creations!

MANGO & JASMINE POPSICLES

You can either eat these on their own or use them in a cocktail and create a popsicle cocktail. Here, I have paired a mango popsicle with a jasmine daiquiri for a fun twist (see opposite). The mango popsicles can be eaten separately while sipping the cocktail or it can be left to melt slightly in the cocktail to add extra flavour and then eaten.

2–3 tbsp Brown Sugar Boba (see page 23) or popping boba

120 ml/½ cup freshly brewed jasmine tea

280 g/10 oz. fruit purée (ready-made or see recipe on page 20)

6–8 popsicle moulds

Makes 6-8

1 Spoon half the boba into the base of 6–8 popsicle moulds.

2 Combine the tea with the fruit purée, then spoon on top of the boba.

3 If you would like a more even distribution of boba, you can fill the mould three-quarters full, then freezer until just starting to set so the boba do not sink. Top with more boba and fill to the top with purée.

4 Push the sticks into the moulds, cover and transfer them to the freezer to set.

Note: If you are eating the popsicle on its own, you might prefer to use half fruit purée and half yogurt or kefir to help balance out the sweetness of the purée. I would not recommend using yoghurt in the popsicles for cocktails as this will melt into the drink. Experiment with different flavour combinations or try some of the suggestions on page 91.

Serving suggestion: Make a Jasmine Daiquiri by combining 200 ml/scant 1 cup freshly brewed jasmine tea with 100 ml/scant ½ cup rum, 10 tablespoons Simple Syrup (see page 16) and 30–40 ml/2–3 tablespoons lime juice in a cocktail shaker with ice. Stir to cool slightly, then taste and adjust the sweetness and alcohol quantities if needed. Shake for a minute to mix, then pour into 2 glasses and add a Mango and Jasmine Popsicle (see opposite) and a lime twist to serve.

FRUIT & YOGURT POPSICLES

120 ml/½ cup freshly brewed jasmine tea
280 g/10 oz. fruit purée (see page 20)
150–200 g/⅔–1 cup yogurt or kefir
honey or sweetener, if needed
2–3 tbsp popping boba or Brown Sugar Boba
   (see page 23)

Makes 6–8

1 Combine the tea with the purée. Mix the yogurt or kefir with honey if needed to sweeten.

2 Put the boba in the base of 6–8 popsicle moulds, then add some yogurt to each. You can add this in different quantities, so all look slightly different.

3 Top with the fruit mixture. You could also add the yogurt first, then boba, followed by the tea. Transfer the moulds to the freezer until frozen.

Note: You can also make this recipe without the tea and just add more yogurt and purée.

THAI TEA POPSICLES

150–200 g/⅔–1 cup plain yogurt
2–4 tbsp condensed milk, to taste
2–3 tbsp Brown Sugar Boba (see page 23)
400 ml/1⅔ cups Thai tea (made with 2 Thai tea bags)

Makes 6–8

1 Mix the yogurt with the condensed milk and taste for sweetness.

2 Put the boba in the base of 6–8 popsicle moulds and add some yogurt to each. You can add this in varying quantities, so they all look slightly different.

3 Top with the Thai tea. You could also add the yogurt first, then boba, followed by the tea. Transfer the moulds to the freezer until completely frozen.

BUTTERFLY THYME LEMON POPSICLES

300–400 ml/1¼–1⅔ cups lemonade
2 tbsp Thyme Syrup (see page 19)
2–3 tbsp Brown Sugar Boba (see page 23)
150–200 ml/⅔–1 cup butterfly pea tea

Makes 6–8

1 Combine the lemonade with the thyme syrup and taste.

2 Put the boba in the base of 6–8 popsicle moulds and top with the lemonade. If you want to see some layering in this, then put the popsicles in the freezer at this stage and leave to semi-set slightly. How long this will take will depend on the temperature of your freezers, so check every 30 minutes. What you want is for a thin layer of ice to form on the lemonade so when you add the tea, it won't sink in and mix.

3 Once slight frozen, top with the butterfly pea tea and freeze again. You can also skip the intermediate freezing and add the tea in straight away to get a purple-coloured lolly.

Flavour suggestions:

Strawberry purée and kefir
Blueberry purée and yogurt
Raspberry purée and kefir
Pineapple purée and coconut yogurt
Peach purée and vanilla yogurt

SUPPLIERS

Below is a list of suppliers that I used when working on this book. Most Asian shops now stock bubble tea supplies, so always check in your local shops to see what is available. Wherever you are in the world, you can also find a lot of things on Amazon.

ASIAN FOOD STORES

Longdan Oriental Supermarket
*Several locations in London
and outside London*
www.longdan.co.uk

Tian Tian Supermarket
Several locations in London
www.tiantian.london

Tawana Thai supermarket
18 Chepstow Rd, London W2 5BD
+44 20 7221 6316
www.tawana-thai.co.uk

ONLINE RESOURCES

UK:
www.orientalmart.co.uk
www.starrymart.co.uk
www.zing-asia.co.uk
www.tradewindsorientalshop.co.uk
www.amazon.co.uk
www.bobaformosa.co.uk
www.bobabuzz.co.uk
www.bobabox.co.uk

US:
www.ntfoods.com
www.bossenstore.com
www.leamaxx.com
www.bobateadirect.com
www.milkteafactory.com

INDEX

ACKNOWLEDGEMENTS

Firstly, I would like to thank Luis Peral for recommending me for this book. It has been such a fun one and working with him on this has been wonderful, as was working with photographer Alex Luck who I would also like to thank.

A big thank you to my assistant Hattie Baker for all your hard work, positive attitude and all the tasting before and during the shoot!

I would like to thank my family and my dear friend Kristina for their constant support and encouragement.

Finally, I would like to thank the entire team at Ryland Peters and Small for entrusting me with this project and helping me bring it to life.